Collies are beautiful, smart, lively dogs

Collies

Anne Fitzpatrick

A⁺

Smart Apple Media

COPYRIGHT

🐏 Published by Smart Apple Media

1980 Lookout Drive, North Mankato, MN 56003

Designed by Rita Marshall

Copyright © 2004 Smart Apple Media. International copyright reserved in all countries. No part of this book may be reproduced in any form without written permission from the publisher.

Printed in the United States of America

🐏 Photographs by Joan Balzarini, Corbis (Tom Nebbia), dogpix.com (Larry Reynolds), Getty Images (Paul Harris, Time Life/Hulton Archive), Tom Myers, Unicorn Stock Photos (Jeff Greenberg, Gary Randall, Ken Schwab)

🐏 Library of Congress Cataloging-in-Publication Data

Fitzpatrick, Anne. Collies / by Anne Fitzpatrick.

p. cm. – (Dog breeds) Summary: Introduces the physical characteristics, life cycle, breeding, training, and care of collies. Includes instructions for an activity related to herding sheep.

🐏 ISBN 1-58340-315-9

1. Collie–Juvenile literature. [1. Collie. 2. Dogs.] I. Title. II. Series.

SF429.C6F58 2003   636.737'4–dc21   2002042810

🐏 First Edition 9 8 7 6 5 4 3 2 1

Collies

Dog Heroes — 6

Growing Up — 12

The Shepherd's Dog — 14

Taking a Collie Home — 18

Hands On: Herding Sheep — 22

Additional Information — 24

CONTENTS

Dog Heroes

Collies became one of the most popular dog **breeds** in the world when a movie called *Lassie Come Home* came out in 1943. The movie's main character was a collie named Lassie, who traveled for many miles through the wilderness to find her family. Lassie's courage and intelligence made people all over the world fall in love with collies. There have been many collie heroes in real life, too. During World Wars I and II, collies carried messages for soldiers in battle. The first Dog

Lassie was first played by a male collie

6

Hero award was given in 1954 to a collie named Tang. He pushed several children out of the path of a car, saving their lives. Today, collies work as **search and rescue dogs**, drug-sniffing police dogs, and guide dogs for blind and deaf people. Collies are as beautiful as they are smart. Their eyes are bright and full of life. They have

A part-collie, part-husky named Chips received a medal from the United States for his service in World War II.

upturned ears and long, narrow noses. The kind of collie most people know is the rough-coated collie. Its coat is long, thick,

Collies' thick coats can be hot in the summer

A special sheepherding dog called a border collie

and soft. A less common type of collie, the smooth-coated collie, has a much thinner coat. Most collies' coats are two or three different colors. They can be black, white, tan, bluish-gray, or brown.

Growing Up

Female collies are pregnant for about two months. They usually have **litters** of three to six puppies. Puppies are blind and deaf when they are born. They spend much of the first few weeks sleeping and **nursing**. When they are five weeks old, collie puppies stop nursing and start eating dog food. At 8 or

10 weeks, they can leave their mother for a new home.

Collies reach their adult size by the time they are two years

old. When full-grown, male collies are about 25 inches (65 cm)

A pair of eight-week-old collie puppies

tall at the shoulder and weigh about 70 pounds (30 kg).

Female collies are about two inches (5 cm) shorter and weigh

about 10 pounds (4 kg) less. Most collies live 12 to 16 years.

The Shepherd's Dog

The collie comes from **sheepherding** dogs in Scotland.

Some people think they may have been mixed with dogs

brought to Britain by the Romans 2,500 years ago. Collies are

excellent sheepherding dogs because of their intelligence and

willingness to work. In 1860, Queen Victoria of England

Collies learn quickly and work hard

saw sheepherding collies in Scotland and fell in love with them. She brought some back to England with her, and the collie soon became a popular pet as well as a valued working dog. The smooth-coated collie was probably used to herd sheep and cattle to the market. Its coat was too thin for the cold, wet weather in which most sheepherding dogs must work. Today, it is useful as a water rescue dog because it is not weighed down by a heavy coat.

Collies with all-white coats do not make very good sheepherders because the sheep think they are sheep too.

Rough-coated collies are warm even when wet

Taking a Collie Home

Collies make excellent pets, especially in families with young children. They are loyal and loving, playful but gentle. Collies are very smart and can be trained easily. Because they become deeply attached to their families and do not like strangers, collies make very good watch-dogs. They are easygoing indoors but full of energy when taken outside. Collies do need a lot of time and care. The long, thick coat of the rough-coated collie must be brushed

Collie dogs were named after colleys, a black-faced type of sheep found in Scotland.

once a week. Collies must get plenty of exercise every day. As

sheepherding dogs, collies are able to run up to 40 miles (15

km) a day. They do not have to run that far every day, but they

Collie pups stay close to their mother

do need to run a lot! Collies also need plenty of food and water to stay happy and healthy. If left alone for too long, collies become bored and may start digging, barking, or chewing on things. If the collie has any fault, it is that it loves people and playing too much! For the family that loves to play with their dog as much as the collie loves playing with people, a collie is the perfect pet.

The dog who played Lassie won the part by crossing a raging river and falling down on the other side.

Collies need a lot of care but give a lot of love

Herding Sheep

Herding sheep is harder than it looks! Collies herd sheep by barking at them, staring them down, and threatening to bite their feet. See how good you are at the collie's job.

What You Need

Three or more friends
A large, open space

What You Do

1. Tell your friends to pretend that they are sheep, and you are a collie.
2. Decide where the sheep pen will be, but do not tell your friends. Real sheep do not know where they are being herded.
3. Try to herd your friends into your imaginary sheep pen. Remember, you cannot talk to them (except by barking) or touch them!

Sheep about to be herded into a pen

Index

care of 18-20

coats 8, 12, 16

heroes 6, 8

history 14, 16

jobs 6, 8, 14, 16

Lassie 6, 20

puppies 12-13

sheepherding 14, 16, 22

sizes 13-14

Words to Know

breeds (BREEDZ)—types of dogs, such as collies, poodles, or bulldogs

litters (LITT-urz)—groups of puppies born at the same time

nursing (NURS-ing)—drinking mother's milk

search and rescue dogs (SURCH and RES-kyoo dogz)—dogs that sniff out people who are missing and bring them back to safety

sheepherding dogs (SHEEP-hurd-ing dogz)—dogs that gather sheep and move them wherever a person wants them to go

Read More

American Rescue Dog Association. *Search and Rescue Dogs*. New York: John Wiley & Sons, 2002.

Knight, Eric M. *Lassie Come Home*. New York: Bantam, 1995.

McKewen, Allene. *The Collie*. New York: John Wiley & Sons, 2000.

Internet Sites

The American Rescue Dog Association
http://www.ardainc.org

The Lassie Network
http://www.lassie.net

The Collie Club of America
http://www.collieclubofamerica.org

INFORMATION